Classic Tales

Level 4

Cinderella

Retold by Sue Arengo
Illustrated by Laure Fournier

 Contents

OXFORD
UNIVERSITY PRESS

Once upon a time there was a good man. He had a good wife and a beautiful, kind daughter. They all lived in a nice old house and were very happy. But one day the man's wife died. And then the man and his daughter were very sad.

After two years, the man married again. His new wife was a nasty woman with a loud voice. She had two daughters. One of them was tall and thin. She was called Prudence. The other daughter was short and fat. She was called Charlotte. Prudence and Charlotte were ugly girls. People called them 'the ugly sisters'.

The man was afraid of his new wife. He said to his daughter, 'I know that you are a good girl. Be kind to your new mother and your new sisters.'

'Yes, Father,' she answered.

But the two ugly sisters hated the man's daughter because she was beautiful and good.

'You can sleep in that little room at the top of the house,' said Prudence. 'And you must do all the work. Give me your nice clothes. Here – you can wear this old dress. And give me your nice shoes. You don't need shoes.'

'Yes,' said Charlotte. 'Start working now! This house is dirty. You must clean it!'

So every day the beautiful, kind girl worked hard. She cleaned the house. She washed and cooked. She made the beds. She did everything!

In the evenings she was tired, so she sat down in the kitchen. She always sat close to the fire and her dress and feet got dirty in the cinders. And so the ugly sisters began to call her 'Cinderella'.

One day a letter arrived. Prudence quickly opened it.

'Oh look, Mother!' she said. 'It's from the king! He is having a big party at the palace for his son, the prince.'

'A party! A party!' said Charlotte.

'Can I come?' asked Cinderella.

'You? Don't be stupid!' said the ugly sisters. 'You can't come. But we will need new dresses. And you must make them for us.'

So Cinderella worked very hard. She made beautiful new dresses for her ugly sisters. And on the day of the party, she worked for them all day. She ran upstairs and downstairs. She never stopped.

At last the ugly sisters were ready. They got into their coach and Cinderella said goodbye to them.

'Have a wonderful time!' she called.

Their coach went up the hill to the palace. Now Cinderella felt very sad. She began to cry. Then suddenly she heard a voice.

'Cinderella! Why are you crying?'

Cinderella looked up and saw a beautiful woman in a white dress. It was a fairy!

'I'm crying because I can't go to the party,' said Cinderella.

'But, Cinderella, you *can* go to the party,' said the fairy. 'I will help you, with my magic wand …

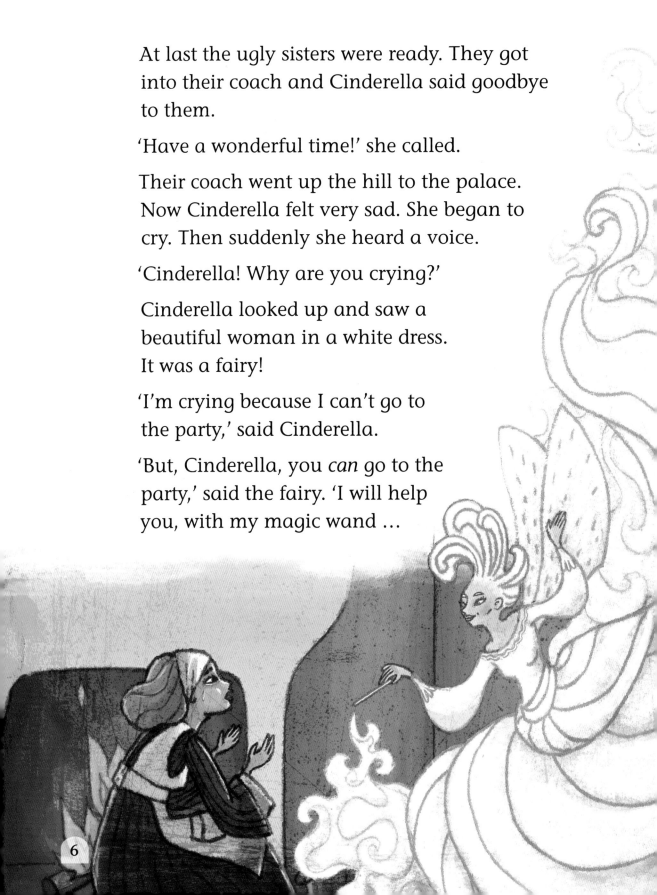

'Listen to me. Go into the garden and bring me a pumpkin.'

'A pumpkin? That's strange!' thought Cinderella. But she ran into the garden and found a big fat pumpkin, and put it on the ground by the fairy's feet.

'Good,' said the fairy. 'Now go and get the mousetrap!'

'The mousetrap? That's strange!' thought Cinderella. But she went and found the mousetrap. There were six white mice in it. She put it on the ground by the fairy's feet.

'One more thing,' said the fairy. 'I need six lizards!'

'Six lizards?' said Cinderella. 'All right! I'll find them!' So she ran into the garden and found six little lizards.

'You *can* go to the party, Cinderella!' said the fairy. 'Watch!'

The fairy touched the pumpkin with her magic wand and suddenly it wasn't a pumpkin! It was a beautiful gold coach – a princess's coach!

Then she touched the six white mice with her magic wand. And suddenly they weren't white mice! They were six beautiful white horses.

Then the fairy touched the six little lizards with her magic wand. And suddenly they weren't lizards! They were six footmen in coats of gold and green and silver.

'Oh, thank you!' said Cinderella.

Then she looked at her dirty old dress.

'But I can't go to the party in this,' she said sadly.

So the fairy touched Cinderella's dress with her magic wand. And suddenly it wasn't a dirty old dress – it was a beautiful long dress with little pink flowers on it. Then the fairy gave Cinderella two little glass shoes for her feet.

'Now. Are you happy?'

'Yes. Oh yes! Thank you!' said Cinderella. 'Thank you!'

'But listen, Cinderella,' said the fairy. 'Before you go, I must tell you something very important. You must leave the party before the clock strikes twelve. Because at twelve o'clock – at midnight – the magic will stop. Then your coach and your horses and your footmen will all go. You will only have a pumpkin, six mice, and six lizards again. And this beautiful dress will go too. You will have your dirty old dress again. Do you understand?'

'Yes,' said Cinderella. 'I understand. I won't forget. Thank you for everything!'

Then Cinderella got into the coach and went to the palace.

When Cinderella arrived at the palace, the prince's footmen were surprised.

'Look at her coach!' they said. 'Look at her dress! Who is she?'

And when she walked into the big room, everyone stopped dancing.

'Who's she?' said Charlotte, the ugly sister. 'Is she a princess?'

'Yes,' said Prudence. 'A very important princess, I think.'

When the prince saw Cinderella, he thought, 'She is the most beautiful girl in the world!' He went to her and said, 'Will you dance with me?'

'Yes,' said Cinderella, 'I will.'

Cinderella had a wonderful time at the party. She danced with the prince all evening and was not tired. But she didn't look at the clock.

At last, she remembered. It was one minute to twelve!

'Oh!' she said. 'It's nearly twelve o'clock! It's nearly midnight! I must go!'

And she ran out of the room.

'Why? Wait!' called the prince. 'Come back! I don't even know your name!'

It was midnight. The clock began to strike twelve o'clock.

Cinderella ran out of the palace and down the stairs. One of her little glass shoes fell off, but she could not stop. So she left it there, on the stairs.

The magic stopped – the fairy was right! Cinderella looked at her dress. Where was her beautiful long dress? Now she had her dirty old dress again. And she had no beautiful coach. There was only a pumpkin. And no horses, and no footmen. Only six white mice and six little lizards, running away into the garden.

Cinderella took off her other glass shoe and put it in her pocket. Then she ran home.

The prince ran out of the palace.

'Where is she?' he said. 'Where is the beautiful princess? Did you see her?'

'No,' answered the footmen. 'We only saw a girl in a dirty old dress, with no shoes. She was a beautiful girl, but she wasn't a princess.'

Then the prince found Cinderella's little glass shoe.

'Here's one of her shoes!' he said. 'I don't know her name, but now I have one of her shoes! I will find her. This shoe will help me. And when I find her, I will marry her.'

The next day the prince's footmen put up an important notice. It said:

Every girl in the country must try on the little glass shoe. The prince will marry the girl who can wear it.

Then the prince and his best footman went to every house in the country. Hundreds of girls tried on the shoe. But it did not fit anyone.

'I will never find her,' thought the prince sadly.

At last, one day, the prince and his footman came to Cinderella's house.

The ugly sisters were very excited. First, Prudence tried on the shoe, but it didn't fit her. Her foot was too long and thin.

Then, Charlotte tried on the shoe. But it didn't fit her. Her foot was much too big and fat.

'Are there any other girls in this house?' asked the prince.

'No!' said the ugly sisters.

'Yes!' said Cinderella's father. 'There's Cinderella. She's in the kitchen.'

'Cinderella?' said the ugly sisters. 'She didn't go to the party. She's only the kitchen girl!'

Cinderella came into the room, in her dirty old dress. But the prince could see that she was very beautiful.

She sat down and tried on the glass shoe. It fitted her perfectly.

'It doesn't fit her! It doesn't!' said the ugly sisters.

'Yes, it does!' said Cinderella's father.

Then Cinderella took the other glass shoe out of her pocket. She put it on her other foot.

'It is you!' said the prince quietly. 'You are the beautiful princess!'

Suddenly there was a great light and the fairy came back. She touched Cinderella's dress with her magic wand, and there was the beautiful long dress with little pink flowers on it!

The ugly sisters and their nasty mother were afraid.

'Oh, Cinderella!' they said. 'We are sorry. We are sorry that we were unkind to you.'

But the prince was very happy. He gave his hand to Cinderella.

'I love you,' he said. 'Will you marry me?'

'Yes, I will,' said Cinderella, 'because I love you too.'

And because Cinderella was kind, she did not forget her ugly sisters.

'Can my sisters come to the palace too?' she asked.

'Yes, they can,' answered the prince.

A few days later, the prince and Cinderella got married. And the ugly sisters got married too. They married two of the prince's friends.

When the people saw Cinderella, they saw that she was very beautiful. And soon they loved her, because she was also good and kind.

After some time, Cinderella and the prince had a little son and a little daughter. And they all lived happily ever after.

1 Circle the correct words.

1 Cinderella ran and found six little **lizards** / **pumpkins**.
2 The fairy touched the pumpkin with her magic wand and suddenly it was a **gold / white** coach.
3 The fairy touched the lizards and suddenly they were **footmen / horses.**
4 The fairy said, 'You must leave the party before **ten / twelve** o'clock.'
5 Prudence tried on the shoe but her foot was too **thin / fat**.

2 Who is speaking? Write the name for 1–4.
For number 5, what does Cinderella say? Write one sentence.

1 'Be kind to your new mother and your new sisters.'   _Cinderella's father_
2 'We will need new dresses. And you must make them for us.'   _____
3 'You can go to the party, Cinderella!'   _____
4 'Wait! Come back! I don't even know your name!'   _____
5 _____   _Cinderella_

3 Complete the sentences with the past tense of these verbs.

have   find   fall   give   ~~run~~   try   be

1   Cinderella _____ran_____ into the garden and _____ a big fat pumpkin.
2   The fairy _____ Cinderella two little glass shoes for her feet.
3   One of Cinderella's little glass shoes _____ off.
4   Hundreds of girls _____ on the shoe.
5   Charlotte's foot _____ much too big and fat.
6   Cinderella and the prince _____ a little son and a little daughter.

4 Write the words.

too ...   dirty   thin   tall   ~~long~~   big   short

1   It's _____too long_____.
2   It's _____.
3   It's _____.
4   They're _____.
5   She's _____.
6   He's _____.

Glossary

cinders small hot pieces from a fire

clock

coach

fairy

fit to be the right size – not too big or too small

footman a man who works for a king or an important person

glass *a glass shoe*

gold *a gold coat*

letter

lizard

magic when things that seem impossible happen

married past tense of **marry**: to become someone's husband / wife

midnight twelve o'clock at night

mouse   **mice**

mousetrap a thing for catching mice

notice a paper for people to see; it tells them important things

palace a king or queen's home

perfectly completely; without any problems

pocket

pumpkin

silver *a silver coat*

stairs

strike to show the time with a noise from a clock

stupid not clever; silly

surprised *She's surprised.*

thin *She's thin.*

top *the top of the stairs*

try on to put on clothes or shoes to see if they fit

ugly not nice to look at

unkind not kind or nice to people

wand

Classic Tales

Classic stories retold for learners of English – bringing the magic of traditional storytelling to the language classroom

Level 1: 100 headwords
- The Enormous Turnip
- The Little Red Hen
- Lownu Mends the Sky
- The Magic Cooking Pot
- Mansour and the Donkey
- Peach Boy
- The Princess and the Pea
- Rumpelstiltskin
- The Shoemaker and the Elves
- Three Billy-Goats

Level 2: 150 headwords
- Amrita and the Trees
- Big Baby Finn
- The Fisherman and his Wife
- The Gingerbread Man
- Jack and the Beanstalk
- Thumbelina
- The Town Mouse and the Country Mouse
- The Ugly Duckling

Level 3: 200 headwords
- Aladdin
- Goldilocks and the Three Bears
- The Little Mermaid
- Little Red Riding Hood

Level 4: 300 headwords
- Cinderella
- The Goose Girl
- Sleeping Beauty
- The Twelve Dancing Princesses

Level 5: 400 headwords
- Beauty and the Beast
- The Magic Brocade
- Pinocchio
- Snow White and the Seven Dwarfs

All *Classic Tales* have an accompanying
- e-Book with Audio Pack containing the book and the e-book with audio, for use on a computer or CD player. Teachers can also project the e-book onto an interactive whiteboard to use it like a Big Book.
- Activity Book and Play providing extra language practice and the story adapted as a play for performance in class or on stage.

For more details, visit
www.oup.com/elt/readers/classictales

OXFORD
UNIVERSITY PRESS

Great Clarendon Street, Oxford, OX2 6DP, United Kingdom

Oxford University Press is a department of the University of Oxford. It furthers the University's objective of excellence in research, scholarship, and education by publishing worldwide. Oxford is a registered trade mark of Oxford University Press in the UK and in certain other countries

© Oxford University Press 2012

The moral rights of the author have been asserted

First published in Classic Tales 1995

2016 2015 2014 2013 2012

10 9 8 7 6 5 4 3

ISBN: 978 0 19 423942 4

This *Classic Tale* title is available as an e-Book with Audio Pack
ISBN: 978 0 19 423945 5

Also available: Cinderella Activity Book and Play
ISBN: 978 0 19 423943 1

Printed in China

This book is printed on paper from certified and well-managed sources.

ACKNOWLEDGEMENTS

Illustrated by: Laure Fournier/The Organisation